A PORTRAIT OF
WINCHESTER

A PORTRAIT OF
WINCHESTER
Capital of Wessex

ALAN HAYWARD

HALSGROVE

First published in Great Britain in 2007

British Library Cataloguing-in-Publication Data
A CIP record for this title is available from the British Library

ISBN 978 1 84114 540 2

HALSGROVE
Halsgrove House, Ryelands Farm Industrial Estate,
Bagley Green, Wellington, Somerset TA21 9PZ
Tel: 01823 653777   Fax: 01823 216796
email: sales@halsgrove.com
website: www.halsgrove.com

Printed and bound by D'Auria Industrie Grafiche, Italy

Contents

Introduction	7	Domestic Architecture	110
Winchester Cathedral	8	Fireworks	124
From River to Castle	42	Ice Skating at Christmas	126
The Hat Fair	76	Christmas Decorations	128
St Catherine's Hill	86	The Hospital of St Cross	132
The River Itchen	102		

King Alfred

Introduction

Winchester holds a special place in the minds of English people for not only was it the first Anglo-Saxon capital of southern central England (Wessex) but it remained the seat of government for its kings and princes. Although its origins are much more distant, the Romans were the first to create a major settlement followed, of course, by King Alfred the Great. So, to generations of school children, from an early age, stories of Roman Britain and King Alfred's Wessex are part of an almost mythical past. The weighty presence of all this history has established Winchester firmly in the national psyche.

Placed at the head of a broad fertile valley with elevated sites for fortification, Winchester was the ideal choice for a defensible settlement. Within easy reach of the sea, it became a major trading town with overseas connections. Trade developed with the rest of the known world through the Roman port of Clausentum (now Bitterne, part of modern Southampton) and established Winchester as a natural seat of government for the region.

Later, in spite of the development of London and its adoption as the nation's capital, Winchester continued to hold the Parliament until the sixteenth century.

Here are all the elements that contribute to our sense of history: a castle, gateways, ruins, winding streets, ancient churches and quiet cloisters set in a wooded valley with river and meadows.

But Winchester is also a modern town beset by all the stresses and pressures common to contemporary town living. It is the county town of Hampshire, seat of local government and public services with a large hospital and a prison, a centre for the arts and a university college. The inevitable pressures and opportunities provided by a good rail link are also felt: the world of the London commuter.

Pressures of population, commerce and traffic are the inescapable consequences of a successful city. But, in spite of these, Winchester retains so many delightful aspects. A quiet river running through, access to nature reserves and open country; these are what linger in my memory. This is a very personal view of Winchester. What should the photographer look for to illustrate the diversity and scale of a city? How broad and inclusive should I make my choice of subject matter? After chasing several themes and subjects, I decided to confine myself to those aspects of the City which are most easily found within a short walk from the centre. These are what remain in the minds of visitors and residents, representing the 'essence' of the City when all the difficulties of access and parking have faded. For Winchester remains a delightfully pleasant place in which to live and to visit.

Winchester Cathedral

The Cathedral is approached from the town across an open grassy area. Popular with townsfolk and tourists, here is a place to relax and enjoy a contrast to the bustle and traffic of the town.

There has been a church on this site since the earliest days of Christianity in this country. The first minster was built in 648 at the command of Cenwald, King of Wessex, and from then on it became a cathedral in which many of the Kings of Wessex and later, of England, were buried.

The outline of the original minster can be seen in the grass on the north side of the present Cathedral.

On the orders of William the Conqueror, this minster was replaced by the Cathedral we see today. Even after many modifications, the Norman architecture predominates.

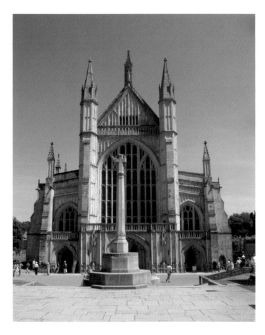

On entering the West Door, the height and length of the nave makes one pause and wonder, for this is the longest cathedral nave in England. Amazingly, the vaulted stonework ceiling, set on huge pillars, seems so solid and yet the whole structure is supported by a timber structure hidden above it. Then, above that, there is a lead covered roof of almost nine hundred square metres.

The Great West Window deserves a close look, for although it is an ancient and original part of the building, it is curiously modern in the abstract patterns of its stained glass. The reason for this contrast is that during the English Civil War, Parliamentary troops reputedly used the window for target practice.

Following its destruction, the shattered pieces of glass were carefully collected and saved until 1660 when they were placed in their seemingly random mosaic. Consequently, the window has become a symbol of the renewal and regeneration that can come from war.

On the south side of the Nave is the chantry chapel of William of Wykeham, one of the most significant figures in the history of Winchester. From humble origins, he was successful in managing church business, became influential in politics as keeper of the Privy Seal and the King's private secretary. He was appointed Bishop of Winchester 1366 – 1404 and in this role he renewed the fabric of the Cathedral. He was a pioneer in educational thinking and founded the now famous boys school, Winchester College and New College, Oxford. Round his tomb runs the well known motto 'Manners makyth man'.

Across the Nave is the twelfth-century font of black marble from Tournai in Belgium. One of seven in England, it consists of a square bowl on five pillars. Its four sides are decorated with medallions of symbolic doves, foliage and flowers, together with illustrations from the legend of St Nicholas, patron saint of sailors and children.

In Memory of
JANE AUSTEN,
youngest daughter of the late
Rev.ᵈ GEORGE AUSTEN,
formerly Rector of Steventon in this County.
she departed this Life on the 18ᵗʰ of July 1817,
aged 41, after a long illness supported with
the patience and the hopes of a Christian.

The benevolence of her heart,
the sweetness of her temper, and
the extraordinary endowments of her
mind obtained the regard of all who
knew her, and the warmest love of her
intimate connections.

Near to the font, set in the floor is Jane Austen's grave. Strangely, no mention is made of her skill and reputation as a novelist, only of her attractive personality. The brass plaque on the wall puts matters right by commemorating her writing: it was paid for with the proceeds from her first biography.

In the Crypt, a figure stands. This is one of several works by the sculptor Antony Gormley based on his own body.

The Quire is probably the finest of the medieval quires to have survived in England.
Its detailed carvings depict scenes and personalities from life, foliage and mythical beasts.

The High Altar and Great Screen were largely rebuilt in Victorian times following desecration during the Reformation.

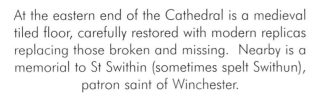

At the eastern end of the Cathedral is a medieval tiled floor, carefully restored with modern replicas replacing those broken and missing. Nearby is a memorial to St Swithin (sometimes spelt Swithun), patron saint of Winchester.

A line of modern icons hangs on the
rear of the High Altar screen.

Surrounding the Presbytery, high on the walls
are several relic boxes which contain bones
of the ancient kings and bishops of Wessex.

It is unusual to find the figure of Joan of Arc in an English cathedral, but here she is standing looking across at Cardinal Beaufort's Chantry. He was her persecutor and responsible for ordering her death by burning in Rouen.

Also, seemingly out of place, is the figure of a diver complete with his heavy primitive diving suit and holding his helmet. This is to commemorate William Walker who, early in the last century, almost single handedly saved the Cathedral from collapsing. The ancient timber foundation had become rotten and unable to support the weight of the walls. Working alone and under water in the dark for several years, he carefully removed the old timbers and replaced them with sacks of cement.

At the eastern end of the Cathedral is a delightful path leading to the Close.

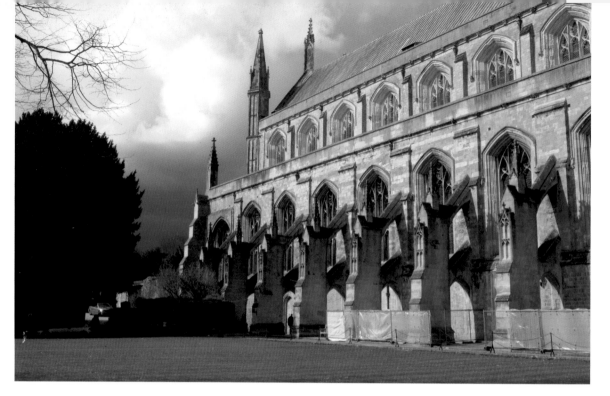

The Close has a quiet calm, encouraging a slower reflective approach to life.

Opposite:
The outside wall of the south transept shows how the cathedral was once attached to the buildings of St Swithun's Priory.

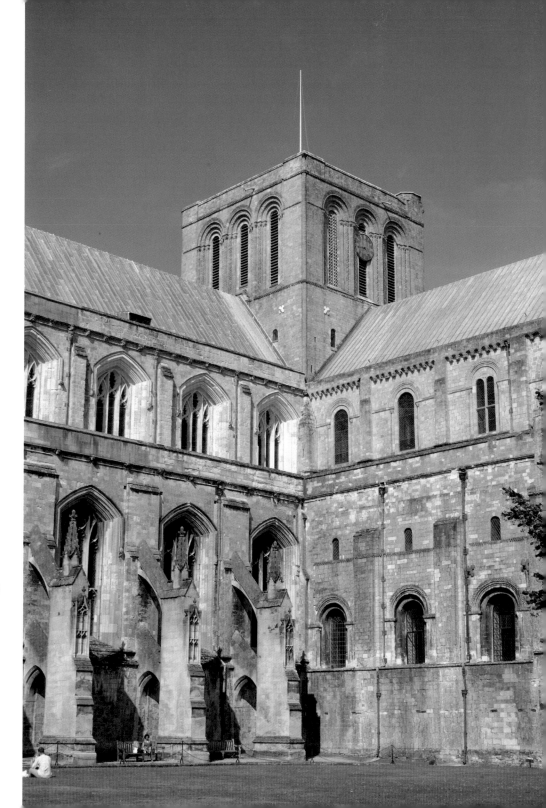

By the Deanery is the garden commemorating Thomas Garnier who was
Dean of Winchester 1840 – 1872 and a distinguished horticulturalist.

Opposite: Here is a peaceful place to relax; a favourite place for gardeners and artists.

The thirteenth-century porch.

Opposite:
Phillip of Spain stayed here in the
Deanery before his marriage to
Mary Tudor in the Cathedral in 1554.
Rebuilt after the Civil War, it was
extended so that Charles II
could entertain his guests.

The residence of the Bishop of Winchester and his staff, Wolvesey was once part of a much larger building with a castle nearby built by the Anglo-Saxon King Ethelwold in the tenth century.

Wolvesey can be seen from St Giles's Hill.

The late sixteenth-century Cheyney Court by the entrance to the Close is where the Bishop held his court.

The Priory Gate with its nail studded door was
the main entrance to the Close. A high wall
surrounds this part of the Close reminding
us of its enclosed and exclusive past.

Above the gate, with the Cathedral's Coat of Arms, is a house designed originally for the Cathedral organist.

Kingsgate, close to the Priory Gate, was originally one of the Roman gates to the City.
Above it is the tiny church of St Swithun.

Known as Jane Austen's house, this is where the novelist lived with her sister and to be near her doctor for the last six weeks of her life.

Winchester College was established by Bishop William of Wykeham in 1387 and has become
one of the premier public schools in the country. The high wall perhaps suggests its exclusivity.

The War Cloister is a moving memorial to the former pupils of the College (known as Wykehamists) killed during the First World War. At its centre is a stone column of a cross with two crusaders.

HERE
IN EQUAL HONOUR
FACING THE NAMES
OF THE FALLEN IN THE
FIRST WORLD WAR
ARE INSCRIBED
THOSE OF THE TWO
HUNDRED & SEVENTY
WYKEHAMISTS
WHO DIED SERVING
IN THE SAME FAITH
1939·1945

Near the Close and College, there are many interesting houses with distinctive features in the network of narrow streets. These are best enjoyed on foot.

From River to Castle

In complete contrast to the built areas, a short walk north from the town is the Winnal Nature Reserve. Here the river valley has been preserved undeveloped: a reminder of what the valley might have been like in the past.

Even in the winter this is a pleasant
open space much enjoyed by walkers
and especially anglers.

Following the River Itchen to the south,
although surrounded by houses, the river
bank is kept as open parkland.

Dominating the eastern side of the town, St Giles's Hill provides a panorama of the City centre.
It is best enjoyed when the trees have lost their heavy canopy of leaves. During the Middle Ages,
because of the prosperous cloth trade, a fair was held here with merchants coming from all over Britain
and Western Europe. King Alfred's statue and the Guildhall are here in the centre of the City.

On top of St Giles's Hill there was an Iron Age fort of the Belgae tribe. This area known as Oram's Arbor was fortified by the Romans 43 – 70AD.

A plaque tells us that Bishop Swithun
had the first bridge over the
River Itchen built here in 859.

The City Mill, built here in 1744 and recently restored by the National Trust, used the fast-flowing river to process grain and cloth. There has been a mill here for over 900 years. Otters are now regular visitors.

Just below St Swithun's Bridge
is the only remaining part of the
Roman Wall. The Romans established
a town they named Venta Belgarum,
meaning the market place of the
Belgae. It extended over 140 acres
with a grid pattern of streets
around the High Street we see today

The river was divided into two streams to reduce the risk of flooding. Here it flows through the Abbey Gardens.

Alfred was King of Wessex from 871-899 and responsible for fortifying the town against the Vikings. So his imposing statue, erected in 1901 to commemorate his millenary, rightly stands looking proudly upon his inheritance.

Abbey House is the official residence of the Mayor of Winchester. It is built on the site of the original monastery which was demolished by Henry VIII.

Opened in 1873, the Guildhall is
built in an elaborate gothic revival style.
Originally constructed to house local
government, law courts, museum,
library and police station, the Guildhall
is now an extensive conference venue
with excellent catering and
exhibition facilities.

St John's House stands near King Alfred's statue. Now used for church worship, in the past it was a venue for entertainment and social gatherings. For instance, the composer and pianist Franz Lizst gave concerts here.

Remains of the anglo-saxon minster for nuns were found by the Guildhall in Abbey Passage.

The High Street, once the main thoroughfare of the City is now a pedestrian area.
This part, known as the Pentice was the Royal Mint until 1279.

The fifteenth-century Buttercross
stands tucked into a corner of
the High Street. A popular meeting
place, it is rarely seen unoccupied
by folk enjoying an elevated view
of the passing scene.

Through the passage by the
Buttercross is the site of William
the Conqueror's palace. Here is
the modest church of St Lawrence
where traditionally the Bishops
of Winchester have visited to pray
before their enthronement.

Known as The Square, the whole of this area was covered by the Royal Palace. Later it became
a cattle market and a site of public executions, notably the execution of Dame Alice Lisle,
sentenced by Judge Jeffries for harbouring loyalist sympathisers during the Civil War.

Bollards around the square have been attractively painted in the styles of various artists.

The City Museum has a range of interesting displays from Roman Mosaics to reconstructions of Victorian and early twentieth-century shops. Workshops for parents and children are popular.

The clock is a distinctive feature
of the High Street on the Old Guildhall.

In common with most towns, the High Street is dominated by large established chains of retailers. The variety of small businesses and shops that distinguished one town from another has almost disappeared. These offices of the local newspapers represent that era, but how long will they last?

The God Begot House, although sixteenth century, gets its name from the manor established by Queen Emma, wife of King Canute, in 1052.

To the east of the High Street Is an area known as 'The Brooks'. Here is the main central car park where occasional farmer's markets are held.

Looking up the High Street towards the Westgate is the area known as The Castle.

Once part of the city wall, the twelfth-century Westgate was rebuilt in the fourteenth century with portcullis and embrasures, mainly in anticipation of attack from France. It now houses a small museum.

Climbing to the top of the
Westgate, this is the view
looking east across the City to
St Giles' Hill. On the site of the
original Norman castle, rebuilt
by William the Conqueror as the
seat of government for the Norman
kings, the administrative offices
of Hampshire County Council
now stand. The Norman castle
was demolished after the
Civil War in 1651.

This is the entrance to the Great Hall, which together with the ruins and passageways nearby, are all that remain of the original castle.

The Great Hall is where important ceremonial events took place from Norman times. King William II (William Rufus), killed in the New Forest in a hunting accident, would probably have been laid in state here before his burial in the Cathedral.

The Round Table has hung here for 600 years. Legend suggests it is King Arthur's. It was painted in Henry VIII's reign with King Arthur given Henry's face. When the Royal Court had moved to London, the Great Hall was used as a Court of Law until the 1970s. Here Sir Walter Raleigh was condemned to death and the notorious Judge Jeffries held his assize. Here, he sentenced Dame Alice Lisle to be beheaded.

This magnificent bronze statue of Queen Victoria was made for her Jubilee in 1897 and originally stood by the Westgate and then in the Abbey Gardens.

The stainless steel gates were commissioned to celebrate the marriage of the Prince and Princess of Wales in 1981.
On the wall are listed the names of every Member of Parliament for Hampshire from 1283 to 1868.
The medieval garden, reconstructed in 1986, is named after England's two Queen Eleanors.

Full of local symbolism representing the ancient history and geography of the area, this sculpture was designed by local sculptor Rachel Fenner to commemorate the Jubilee of the Queen's Coronation in 2003.

The modern Law Courts stand adjacent to the Great Hall. This hog, emblem of the County, is etched onto a large window looking out towards the Law Courts.

The Hat Fair

The Hat Fair takes place during the first weekend of July. This event is a public celebration of street performers coming from far and wide. The atmosphere is that of a relaxed festival with performers and audience moving around the High Street, Square and Cathedral Green.

But for some it is all too much…

St Catherine's Hill

Although it is not part of the City, no portrait of Winchester can neglect St Catherine's Hill. Overlooking the City from the south, the earliest occupation of the area dates back to an Iron Age hill-fort of approximately 2000BC.

The Hospital of St Cross can be seen to the west.

A group of beech trees at the summit provides welcome shade on a hot day. Excavation of the Iron Age fort suggests that the site was occupied until around 150BC. The foundations of a Norman chapel are nearby.

Also on top of the hill is a maze cut into the turf. Its origin and meaning are unknown. It is thought by some to be a penitential device for blindfolded monks to be punished. The design is similar to that on the floor of Chartres Cathedral in France.

To the east, a broad valley isolates the hill. The M3 motorway is hidden in a cutting below the skyline.

Victims of the plague were buried in pits here on the valley floor to the south.

For centuries, pilgrims have travelled between Winchester and Canterbury
along the Pilgrim's Way. They are commemorated in the National Trail
which skirts the foot of the hill and joins the Itchen Trail into the City.

The 'Winchester Bypass' was built in the 1930s controversially separating St Catherine's Hill from the City. Controversy was renewed by the proposal to route the M3 motorway across the water meadows. After fifteen years of bitter wrangling involving many prominent citizens and confrontations between police and protestors, the road was finally built. Completed in1996, the M3 runs to the east of St Catherine's Hill by means of a gigantic cutting through Twyford Down.

The old bypass was returned to nature using chalk from the Twyford Down cutting, restoring the original profile to the hill. It is difficult to believe that in the recent past, thousands of vehicles daily raced over this view.

Remains of the old railway line can be followed southwards along the Shawford Viaduct. This path provides a high level view for walkers of the broad sweep of the river valley, now a site of special scientific interest.

The River Itchen

Now, in contrast to the noise of the motorway,
the valley of the River Itchen is delightfully peaceful.

The river's course towards the City can be traced from the top of St Catherine's Hill.

Down by the river, the hill dominates the skyline seen here across the College playing fields.

… and from here, closer in to the City.

The river walk is enjoyed by residents and visitors, a haven from the bustle of traffic and commerce.

Built in the twelfth century, Segrim's Mill became an important grain mill.
The existing structure, now apartments, was built in1885.

Domestic Architecture

Winchester is packed with interesting houses from all periods – medieval, Georgian, Victorian and modern.
On the following pages is a selection of some of the most attractive individual buildings,
streets and quirky details, that help to make the City so fascinating.

Fireworks

A spectacular annual display of fireworks with a huge bonfire takes place in the parkland once part of Hyde Abbey where King Alfred and his Queen were finally buried.

Ice Skating at Christmas

A recent innovation is ice skating during December in the Cathedral Close.

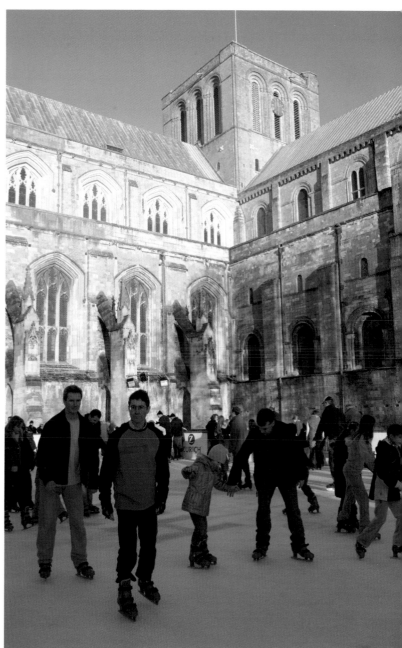

Christmas Decorations

A delightful atmosphere is created in the traffic-free High Street shopping area in the period before Christmas with the decorations and street musicians.

The Brooks Shopping Centre
at Christmas.

The Hospital of St Cross

Although not part of the centre of Winchester, the Hospital of St Cross is an integral part of the historical charm of the City. A pleasant surprise for the weary tourist and busy resident, for this is one of the oldest and best preserved almshouses in the country. It is not just a museum, for it is still the home of 25 elderly men.

Since its foundation in 1136, a home has been provided here for the sick and elderly, and the 'feeding of one hundred poor people a day'. There is also the rule that a traveller should be given bread and ale. This 'Wayfarer's Dole' can still be requested by visitors; a small portion of bread and a beaker of ale, keeping up the 800 year-old-tradition.

The Brethren's Hall is traditionally used for the brother's feasts. Built in 1350, it has a majestic chestnut-beamed roof.

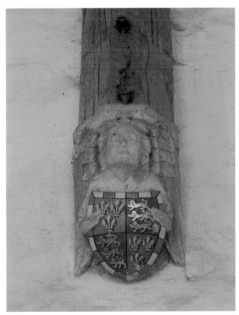

The presence of history is almost palpable. Not that of wars and strife, but of the regular daily routines of eating and sleeping, of society and worship.

The church of St Cross dating from the twelfth century, was the point of departure for crusaders to the Holy Land: a fine example of Transitional Norman architecture.

TO THE GLORY OF GOD AND IN
MOST LOVING MEMORY OF
EMILY MARY (LILLIE) WIDOW OF
NOEL HANBURY. SHE DIED AUG. 21ST 1938

There are many beautiful windows and every pew end is individually carved.

A 'Master' was appointed to oversee the running of the Hospital and installed in this, the 'Master's House'. The incumbents who have enjoyed this title have not always carried out their duties honourably. One, Francis North, during the early nineteenth century stole so much of the Hospital's income that he inspired Trollope's novel *The Warden*.

The Master's garden is a haven of peace. Enclosed, but with views across to St Catherine's Hill.

On past the Hospital of St Cross flows the River Itchen as it has since long before
Winchester ever existed. Here, Keats was inspired to write his 'Ode to Autumn':
'Season of mists and mellow fruitfulness', evoking the timeless character of the valley.